OPOWIEŚĆ O CYFRACH

THE NUMBER STORY

SMALL BOOK ONE

ENGLISH - POLISH

*Numbers Teach Children
Their Number Names*

written and illustrated by

MISS ANNA

Early Reader Edition of *The Number Story 1*
Bronze Medal Winner, 2016 Wishing Shelf Book Award

LUMPY PUBLISHING

Cover by | Lumpy Publishing
Layout by | Lumpy Publishing
Translated by Agnieszka Sarna
Coloring by Jieeun Woo and Maria Mirabella

Library of Congress Control Number: 2018902040

Names: Miss Anna, author.
Title: Number story : numbers teach children their number names / Miss Anna.
Description: Portland, OR: Lumpy Publishing, 2018.
Identifiers: ISBN 978-1-945977-24-4| LCCN 2018902040
Summary: The pictures and rhymes present stories which introduce numbers 0-10.
Subjects: LCSH Numeration—English--Polish--Pictorial works--Juvenile literature. | BISAC JUVENILE NONFICTION /
Languages: English--Polish
Classification: LCC QA141.3 .M57 2018 | DDC 513—dc23

Publisher: Lumpy Publishing
Website: www.missannabooks.com
Email: missanna@missannabooks.com

Paperback: ISBN 978-1-945977-24-4
Printed in the U.S.A.   1 3 5 7 9 10 8 6 4 2

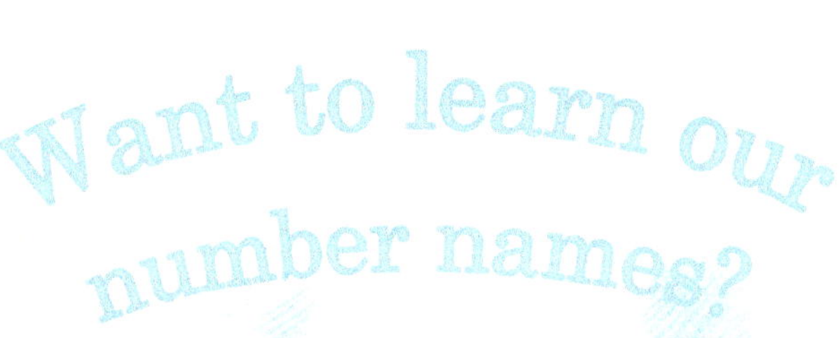

Poznaj z nami
cyfry wszystkie!

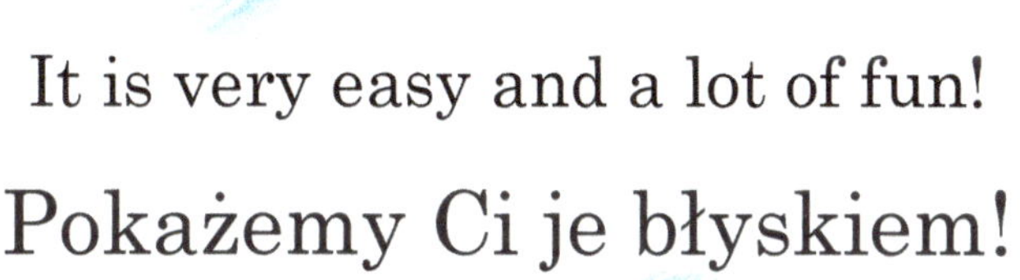

It is very easy and a lot of fun!
Pokażemy Ci je błyskiem!

Say-along our little jingle

Dla Królewny i Rycerza

starting from Number One!

cyfra JEDEN na start zmierza!

1

ONE looks like my one finger.

JEDEN

jak palec zupełnie sam.

ONE!
JEDEN!

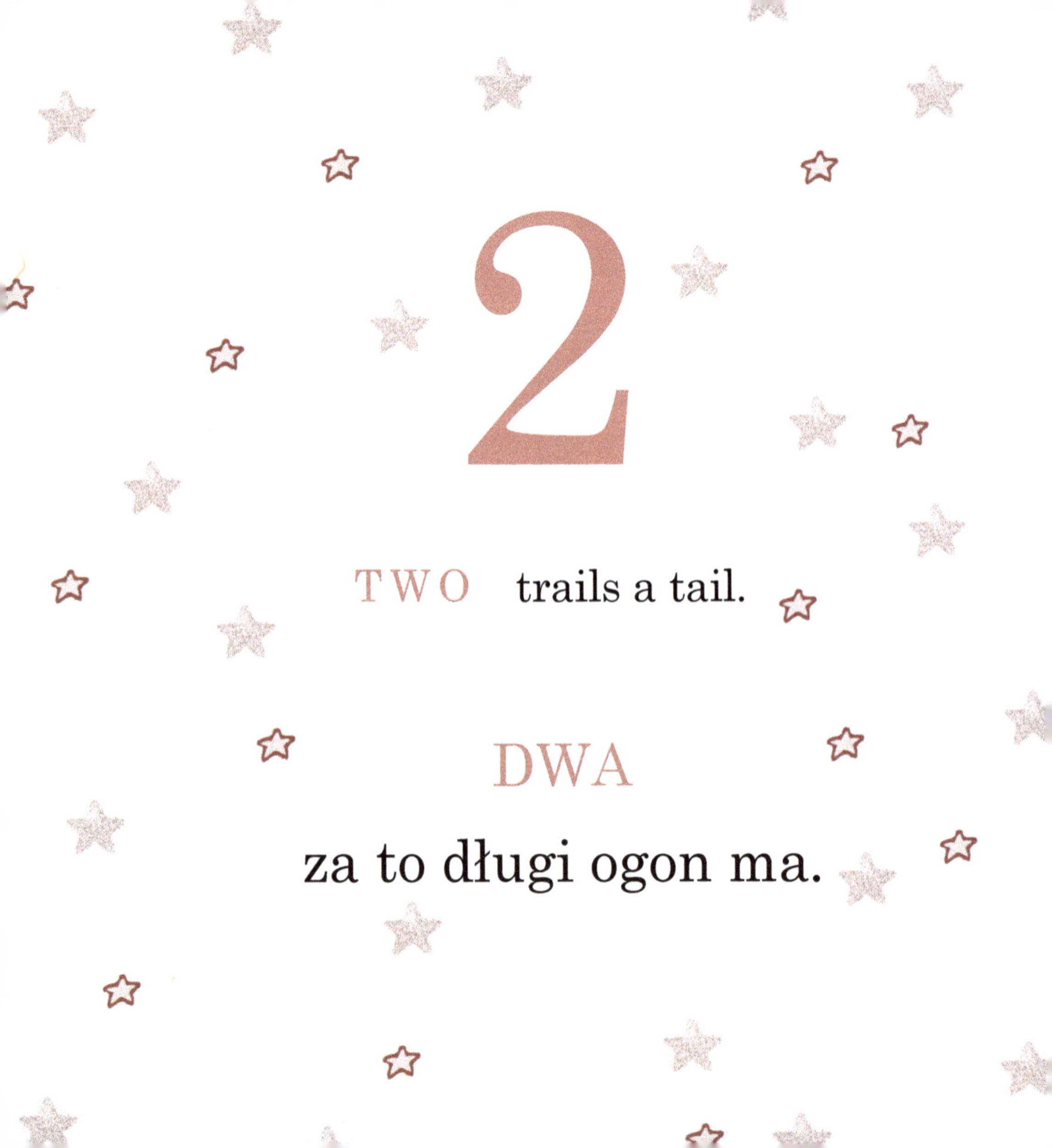

2

TWO   trails a tail.

DWA

za to długi ogon ma.

A TAIL! OGON!

3

THREE has bumps.

TRZY

kocha swe małe garby.

BUMPY! GARBY!

4

FOUR carries a sail.

CZTERY

pokaże żagielek Ci.

A SAIL!
ŻAGIEL!

5

FIVE   is a racing track.

PIĘĆ

będzie ścigać z Tobą się.

VROOM
BRUMBRUM!
1

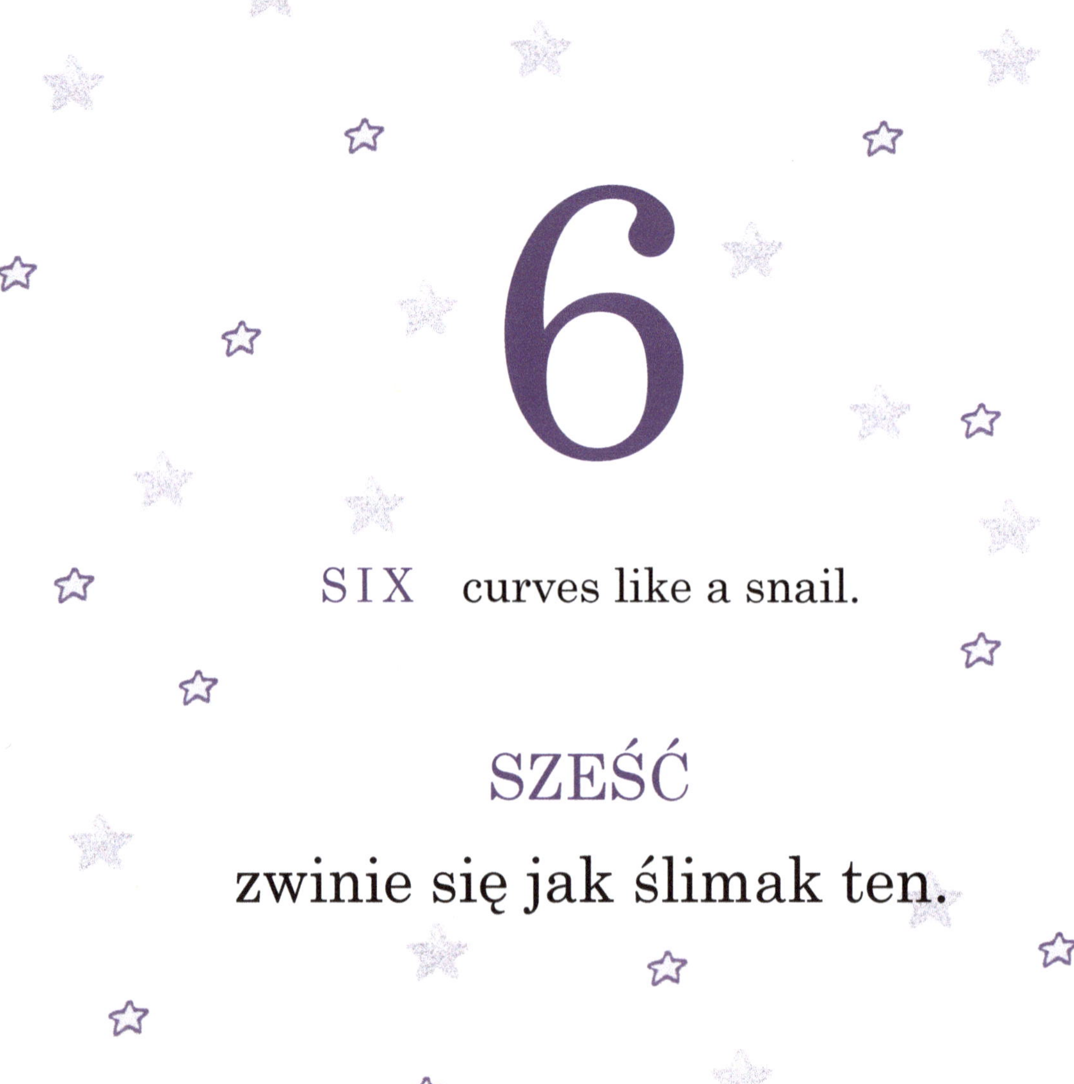

6

SIX   curves like a snail.

SZEŚĆ

zwinie się jak ślimak ten.

A SNAIL! ŚLIMAK!

7

SEVEN has a sharp angle.

SIEDEM

kłujący kąt tu ma.

OUCH!
AU!

8

E I G H T   is rollercoaster rails.

OSIEM

kolejką po torach gna.

HEEEJ!
YIPPEE!

NINE   is a bubble on a stick.

DZIEWIĘĆ

słomka i bańka mydlana!

A BUBBLE! BAŃKA!

TEN is an eye of a whale.

DZIESIĘĆ

wieloryb okiem mruga.

MRUG
MRUG!
WINK!

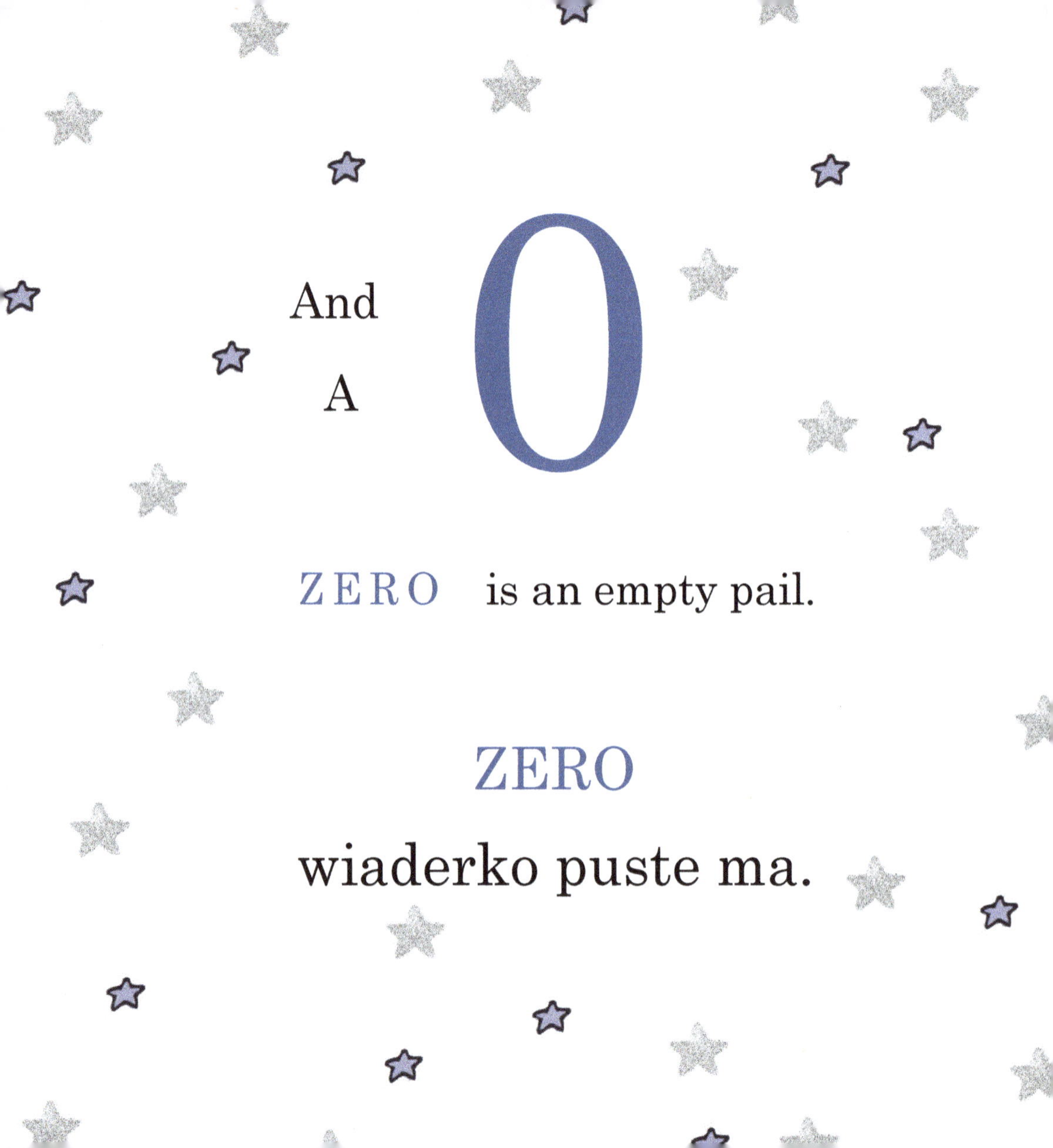

And A

0

ZERO is an empty pail.

ZERO

wiaderko puste ma.

IT'S
EMPTY!

PUSTE!

Thank you for playing with us today.

We had a lot of fun too!

Dziękujemy Wam za dzisiejszą zabawę.

My też świetnie się bawiliśmy!

We are your Number friends,
Zero to Ten,
Who will be here for you~
Jesteśmy Waszymi przyjaciółmi
i pozostaniemy z Wami już zawsze.

Bye-bye now!
See you again soon.
Tymczasem, do widzenia!
Do zobaczenia już wkrótce!

The Numbers are *SINGING* too!

To sing-a-long, look for Miss Anna Number Story
at your favorite music store like iTUNES.

MP3

Numbers 0-10
IDENTIFYING
& COUNTING

Numbers 11-20
& Ordinals

first, second, third...

Numbers 0-100
& Place Values

ones, tens, hundreds...

About Clocks
& Telling Time

hours, minutes, seconds

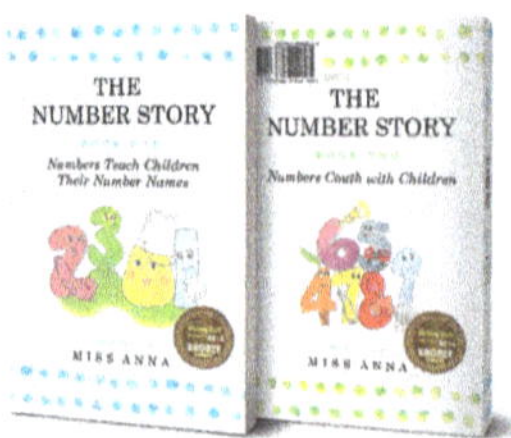

Number Story 1 & 2

isbn: 978-0-996216-48-7

Number Story 3 & 4

isbn: 978-1-945977-01-5

Number Story 5 & 6

isbn: 978-1-945977-06-0

Number Story 7 & 8

isbn: 978-1-949320-40-4

For more Miss Anna books to love,
visit us at

www.missannabooks.com

Numbers are working hard all over the world!
Come Travel the World with Us!